# BREAKING DOWN BARRIERS

# BREAKING DOWN BARRIERS

ON THE INSIDE

in collaboration with CCCF

LUMINARE PRESS
WWW.LUMINAREPRESS.COM

Breaking Down Barriers



Printed in the United States of America
Layout by Nina Leis

Luminare Press
442 Charnelton St.
Eugene, OR 97401
www.luminarepress.com

LCCN: 2022923707
ISBN: 979-8-88679-106-8

*To anyone serving time,*
*your story matters.*

# OUR MISSION

On The Inside builds a creative connection for incarcerated women, both individually and collectively. We do this by telling our stories, igniting our hearts, and sparking dialogue. Creative connection for a greater good, we create community for women on the inside and outside by breaking down the walls that keep us apart.

The United States houses over
1.3 million incarcerated women.
We aim to change that.

# CONTENTS

"You are the artist of your life"

—NIKKI WEAVER,
THE FOUNDER OF ON THE INSIDE

# A MESSAGE FROM THE FOUNDER

"Storytelling, you know, has a real function.
The process of storytelling is itself a healing process...
a form that becomes inseparable from your
whole self. That's what stories do.
Stories differ from advice in that, once you get
them, they become a fabric of your whole soul.
That is why they heal you."

—ALICE WALKER

I've carried this quote around with me for many years, Alice Walker's words help me make sense of what it is I do and why I do it. This book has come together in a way that only stories can, over time we see ourselves in them. We become the fabric of each other's lives and learn to better understand our own. I started writing and drawing stories when I was about five. I would wedge my desk in between my bedroom doorway and sell them to my parents' friends when they would have dinner parties. I would wait for an adult to come over and ask me about what this drawing meant or why I wrote this story. I was always imagining things, worlds, people.

As I grew into adulthood, I was surrounded by books, visual artists, and theatre. I immersed myself in reading, in studying theatre, in seeing films and theatre, in listening to music, in running miles. I wanted to understand how stories lived IN us, and around us. I wanted to consume as many stories as I possibly could. The more I learnt, the more I began to share my own, one small puzzle piece at a time. When the covid pandemic hit, I walked daily for sanity, for exercise, for something to do. This idea was born, to gather stories from those inside side by side those living on the outside; to connect our humanity, to see our similarities, to witness our differences, and ultimately to envision a world where healing might happen collectively.

Thank you for being a part of our story.

—NIKKI WEAVER

FOUNDER, ON THE INSIDE

# ON THE INSIDE

While the nature of our work originally relied on in-person classes, COVID called for us to shift our curriculum to a virtual nature. On The Inside has come together with the women serving time at Coffee Creek Correctional Facility in Wilsonville, Oregon and our civilian community worldwide, to create a book of all of our journeys. Each piece is from the individual's perspective and not a reflection of the views of On The Inside.

On The Inside builds creative connections for women inside prison facilities and outside of prison facilities, both individually and collectively. We do this by telling our stories, igniting our hearts, and sparking dialogue. We offer women the platform to explore themselves, **their** past, **their** present and future. When we come together and see our similarities instead of our differences we create a safe space for healing. We believe each individual has the capacity to heal and grow at their pace and in their own time. We will meet you there. We invite you to join our community!

In the back of the book you can find the author's name and whether or not they were incarcerated, as well as the prompts that were given if you would like to join our healing journey!

Many thanks,
On The Inside

# CONFRONTING THE SELF/HARDSHIP

Is there one belief or recurring thought that you can release in order to cultivate more self-healing?

# MANTRA

The first thing that comes to mind is shame. Guilt is remorse for what you have done, shame is remorse for who you are. Guilt is a healthy means to help us strive to do better. Shame often makes us believe there may be no hope for us. You are always enough! There is always hope.

—ANONYMOUS

# UNNOTICED

I really contemplated writing this or putting myself out there but maybe my truth will help someone else.

In the past two weeks I have been trying to find the reasons why people have to die. I feel like literally my entire life has been surrounded by loss. It's so sad to me. Every time someone close to me has to die I have self medicated to get through to the other side...

Or so I thought.

Really, grief waits for you.

I've been sober for 28 months now and in the last 8 months I've lost my Grandma, my Aunt Janet, and my Uncle Joe who died just days ago. These times I have not self medicated and it seems that all the pain from the past losses have come up for me. I feel like because of my position in life working in the beauty industry (here in prison beauty school). I paint on a smile and put on a big charade when, in reality, I feel like I am suffocating. I have found that dying is a cycle in life everyone eventually goes through, and it hurts the ones left behind.

People have told me it is okay to grieve, but when?

Now, as I'm walking to school or to a call out. Again, I found that grief will wait. The shower is a great time to let it out. Wash up and move on for the day. I have asked myself a thousand times:

"Why do I have to lose so many people in my life?"

"Have I not lost enough?"

"When will I gain."

Yet today it dawned on me, it is the simple things in life that go unnoticed, and everyday I wake up, I have gained...I am one more day sober, still walking through the stages of grief, clean.

—KRISTIE

# UNCERTAIN

Coming from a low income, blended family, with a history of drug abuse and unhealthy relationships. I envisioned myself to "turn out" that way. I was pregnant at the age of 18, facing a decision that I knew would determine the course of my life. The decision I made was one that could be considered selfish. It was for the betterment of myself and not risking the chance of being a single mother with no support or ability to fight for my future. My relationship with my family is tumultuous and shaky. My adoptive dad passed away from alcoholism and my closest family members still struggle with addiction. Over the course of my life I've found it difficult to "prove myself" even to people who don't have a say in my life. It's been an uphill battle to constantly feel like I'm making the right decisions in everyone else's eyes. I've always felt that I am living life as someone looking in, hoping that I'm making decisions that would be deemed good enough by friends, family, and co—workers. There's a piece of me that still feels like I'll always be a low income kid struggling to find acceptance and stability. I often feel embarrassed about how I used to dress/behave and who I would associate with, and sometimes it still feels very much a part of my identity. Even though I try to block it out and not be so enveloped in those feelings. I think the lies that I would want to let go of are that I'm not good enough for good things, and that I don't deserve to be happy, healthy, and at peace with my life and my decisions. As I get older and with the help and support of loved ones and therapy, heavy therapy, I'm learning to let go and unlearn those behaviors and thoughts.

—MIRANDA

When is a time in your life that you didn't get the support you needed?

# UNTITLED

The time I needed family support but didn't get it was when I needed to leave my husband. Everyone had their opinion. They all knew it was a bad situation. Nobody cared to do anything more than talk. I was stuck. First with two kids, then three. I needed to work but couldn't afford daycare for two young children. My mom didn't work. Why was I struggling to leave because I couldn't afford daycare when my mom was totally available? My dad's home had an extra bedroom that at one time was lived in by my sister and another time by my step-sister. The availability of that bedroom doesn't exist when you come with kids. Nobody wanted to visit if he was there. I recall preparing Thanksgiving dinner wondering if anyone would even show up because he was there. The police even had something to say but couldn't help me. **Words.** That's all anyone had to offer. Remember the chant from our childhood that went, "sticks and stones can break my bones but words can never hurt me?" Their words could have been encouraging if actions had followed. Their words alone caused me mental anguish. I knew I needed to leave for me and my kids. I also felt I needed to please people in my life. That feeling caused me to rush and make many mistakes. Many moves, constant job changes. Crashing mental health. I tried and tried for many years. I legally became divorced but I was still trapped. He continued to cause turmoil in my life in many ways. Drunk harassment, financial instability, threats. I still struggled every single day. My anger boiled over and became thunderous thoughts. The words from family and friends became kindling to a fire burning inside me. I said I'd kill him. I said how I'd kill him. Their words fanned the flame. **My words.** My murderous thoughts. Jokingly making plans to rid myself of this constant issue in my life. A third party that didn't care for me caught wind of comments made. She involved the police. The same police who shared words in the past were now arresting me. My words put me in jail. The intent, not attempt, put me in prison. The DA said I had the means to do it. Who doesn't?! 90 months. 7.5 years. Attempted murder. Words have been a force of destruction in my life. I wish they had given me a few less words and a lot more support when I needed it so many years ago.

—TANYA

# STRENGTH

I had a traumatic incident where I felt completely misunderstood and not supported. I had a nervous breakdown due to mounting stress and failing a drug test for weed at a job I loved and had worked very hard at advancing in. My work was supportive, my family was a different story. I called my Brother-in-law late one night, he told me "You have to know who you can trust". That statement had a huge impact on me. I had to learn to listen to the tiny voice inside me saying "this person doesn't have my best interest at heart". I had to listen to that voice and seek support elsewhere. If I learned I had no one to trust I would have to seek support outside my circle. That support and guidance is out there somewhere and I should keep asking and never give up. I had to become my fiercest advocate. I trusted my version of a higher power and I am convinced there is something in the universe or our human connection that is rooting for me. I survived and came back stronger.

—ANONYMOUS

# WHY TRY

You said things would be different.
They seem the same to me.
Asking people I don't know for help.
Is pretty lame to me.
Maybe, we'll see, probably.
I was just a kid.
WHY TRY!

—TANUIA

# SILENT KISSES

December 17, 1996 was the first time in my life that I didn't get the support I needed and it just got worse from there. I was 12 days into my 7 short little years of life when my mom was taken from me for no reason other than sheer selfishness, and to this day I still don't quite understand. My mom did daycare, so in my house growing up during the day it was full of laughter and kids running around. When night fell, there was yelling, crying, the sound of clothes being torn, holes in the walls and doors, and the occasional open hand or fist making contact with another's skin. But despite what my mother had been put through the night before, she'd still wake up each morning to make sure I was up and ready for school. The days leading up to December 17th seemed to just get louder and worse, and then… I woke up on that dreadful day to be completely quiet. There was no sound, so I got ready for school by myself and went to say bye to my mom who was still in bed and I gave her a kiss. The feeling on my lips was cold so I covered her up and left for school. Hours later, our pastor came and picked me up from school to take me home, where he'd try to explain to me that my mom, my protector, had gone to be with my grandma and was already gone when I'd kissed her goodbye earlier that very morning. Days passed and I was kept home from school, and then the day of my mother's funeral arrived. I didn't quite know how to feel, I was sad and felt so alone, but I was also so full of fear. What was going to happen to me? Who was going to take care of me? I thought I could solve that question on my own. I got into the casket with my mom and closed the lid. Problem solved… everyone was so involved with everything else going on that it took at least one hour before anyone noticed that I was even gone. At that very moment, I felt as though I didn't belong anywhere. The state homes for children who have lost their parents will normally check up on the child. However, I was placed in a home where I was reminded that I was only there for them to collect a check. I wasn't allowed to speak of my mother. In fact, I remember the first night I was in their home. I had a nightmare and I was crying out for my mom and my foster dad entered my room, slapped me across the face, and said she didn't exist anymore so I should get over it. I was forced to do all the chores- but nothing I did was good enough. I felt like a real-life Cinderella without the happily-ever-after. I don't recall ever seeing a social worker in what I'd consider to be the worst 12 years of my life. Living and serving my sentence at Coffee Creek has been easier than living with that family.

This was the time I needed support, and it was nowhere to be found.

—MORGAN

# A TIME OF NO SUPPORT

Looking back over my life took a minute for me to find the times when I was not supported. I tried to find people to name, maybe even to blame, but the only person I could identify was myself. Through the rough patches, my addiction, the death of my sister and step dad, my criminal behavior and prison stays, I found I did not support myself. I did not try to lift myself up. I didn't love who I was, let alone like who I had become. It was a lonely time led by unknown fear and anxiety. Because the only emotion I knew was anger I turned my fear into anger. My anxiety became anger and I raged inside to the point of hate. It came to a boiling point where it was fight or flight with myself. I wanted to win. Winning was gaining back my life. Having the freedom within to just be at peace. Today I am my own biggest fan. I found it shows people what I want for myself and what I am willing to accept in my life.

—KRISTIE JEFFERS

What does fear look or feel like?

# PRISON

Fear is a prison. A prison whose walls grow thicker as time goes on. It starts as a warning system, alerting us to danger, but as it is fed, it grows. Fear takes our hopes, steals our dreams, ruins our relationships, sucks our breath out and isolates us. Fear is used and manipulated to control us. Until one day we are looking out onto the world through nothing but fear.

A shell of who we used to be, of who we're meant to be. Capable of things we never thought possible. Yet fear makes us think that what we are doing is needed to protect or just lesser of the two evils. Fear distorts, it persuades and we feed it. The people we allow in our lives, the places we go, the very things we read or watch. These very discreetly feed the fear. It eventually overruns us. No one is immune. Fear is universal. Its walls aren't concrete and steel, barbed wire and razor wire; they are stronger. Held together by the prisoners' own mind. It twists every interaction and every sight into the person's own personal own mind. It twists every interaction and every sight into the person's own personal horror. Your own mind becomes your worst enemy.

What do you do that feeds your fears?

What do you do that feeds someone else's fears?

Change those things and you can begin to free yourself from prison no one should ever be in. Free your mind and the rest will follow.

—KYLA

# FROZEN

Can't move. Can't talk
Afraid to walk
Feels like someone
Sitting on top
Extreme chest pain
Not sure what
He will gain
Fear is pain
Life will never
Be the same

—MEGAN

# FEAR FEELS LIKE

Refusing to lose in times of defeat, maintaining determination know matter the consequences I may receive.

My heart, mind, and soul are always protected by armor, unable to feel the unconditional love, faith, and trust given by my heavenly father. Sitting alone in the unknown. Never feeling the touch of my soulmate again. Still not capable of understanding how we ended so far apart.

Fighting to go free, and failing as a mom.

Passing on cycles of addiction and destruction, never being able to forgive myself for the pain I've caused. Lovinging unconditionally but never feeling worthy of the same in return. Feeling as if my heart has been ripped from my chest so I end up laying down to die, knowing I'll forever be broken inside.

—MICHELLE

# TREPIDATION

Fear,
Feels like suffocation,
Always running and hiding
but it never seems to be
Enough...

Fear,
Like a spot of mold quickly
Spreading like wildfire, running
A precious, growing fruit
Destroying a path of upcoming
Beauty...

Fear,
A cruel motivator, look what's behind the big scary beast.
A shadow hovering, blocking the light.

Question Fear
Ask it what and why...
Shove some light back in its eye.
What once was wild,
is now controlled just for a moment until it sees you
slip.

Fear,
Be open, be mindful, always question what's behind it
It can only go one of two ways
Make you
Or break you.

—MIREYA

# STILL.

When I was living with my kids I had a fear that I would die and leave my kids behind. My oldest, Destiny, has a different dad and is 10 years older than her brothers, Joshua and Jacob. I was scared that if I died that they'd lose touch. I'm now in prison. Alive, but my fears have become reality. My daughter rarely sees her brothers. My fear now isn't about being dead and not being there for my kids. My fear is being alive and not having a relationship with them. Jacob was 6 when I was arrested, and Joshua was 7 ½. I will be incarcerated for 7 ½ years. More time away from them than I had with them. Destiny was 17 ½ when I left. I had so much to teach her still. She has never had a job. She stopped going to school. She's falling into depression and I can't pull her out. What does fear look like? Look at a mother in prison. What does fear feel like? I don't know; I'm numb.

—TANYA SCHMALZ

# REDEFINING THE SELF

What in your life do you choose to challenge?

# WITHIN THE STRUGGLE

How much time is spent asking why?
Why don't things go the way we think they should?
Why does someone we love get sick?
Why are there children born to struggle?
Why are some lives cut shorter than others?
Why so much violence in the world?
Why are things settled in war?
Why so much pain and suffering?

When it occurred to me
We spend so much time focusing on why and fairness,
On being hurt or angry
That we don't see and give thanks for what
Our struggles and disappointments also bring us.
To start with, they bring us words like
Hope and faith
They build characters like courage and strength
They give us feelings like compassion and love
They bring others into our lives that change us
And us into someone else's life that can learn from us.
Our lives are not full because of a lack of struggles and disappointments
Our lives are full because of them and the riches they add to them.
Not riches of silver or gold, but of humanity.

—MICHELLE

# CHAOS

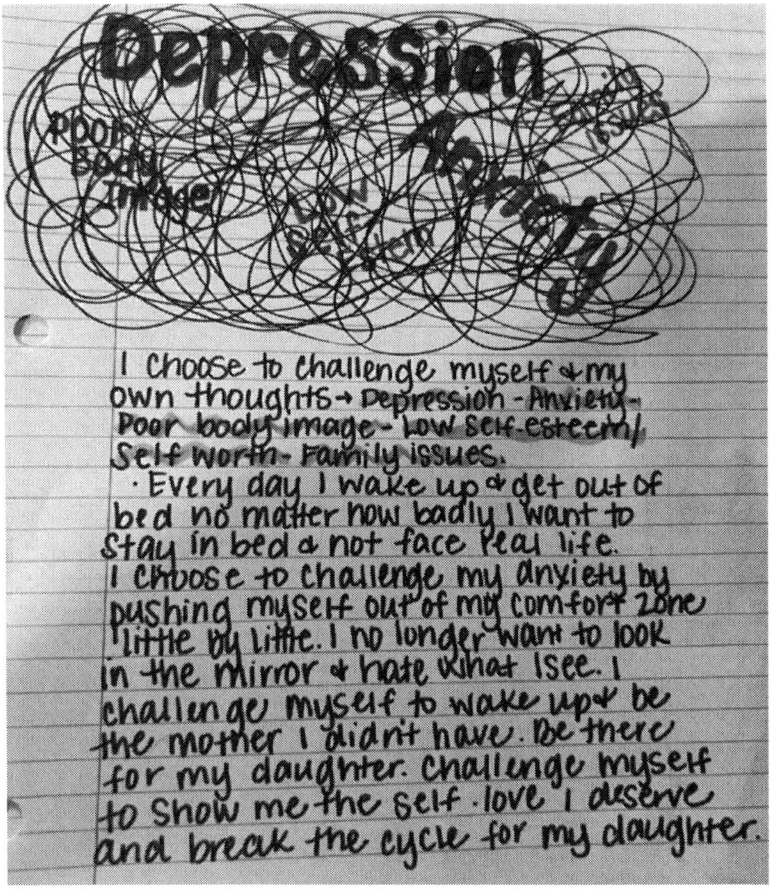
Depression
Poor Body Image
Anxiety

I choose to challenge myself & my own thoughts → Depression - Anxiety - Poor body image - Low self-esteem/ Self worth - Family issues.

· Every day I wake up & get out of bed no matter how badly I want to stay in bed & not face real life.

I choose to challenge my anxiety by pushing myself out of my comfort zone little by little. I no longer want to look in the mirror & hate what I see. I challenge myself to wake up & be the mother I didn't have. Be there for my daughter. Challenge myself to show me the self-love I deserve and break the cycle for my daughter.

# THERE'S NO EXCUSE NOT TO GROW

High mountain tops and valley's low,

There's no excuse not to grow.

A front row seat where I'm the star of the show,

There's no excuse not to grow.

Many trials yet few successes,

Things don't always go right,

What a mess this is.

Yet the lights shine bright and I'm prepared for every lesson.

What will today's trials have me test in?

We are not mere human beings but

Human becomings I want you all to know,

Bottom line.

There is no excuse not to grow.

—TANUIA

# I CAN SEE NOW

There are so many reasons to
Remain in the fight for joy and peace.
No more excuses why perseverance
And do not come first,
Knowing when something great is going
To come out of something stressful
Is a gift.
I've had this gift all of my life.
I can see now that I had to grow into it.
I can see now.

—ANONYMOUS

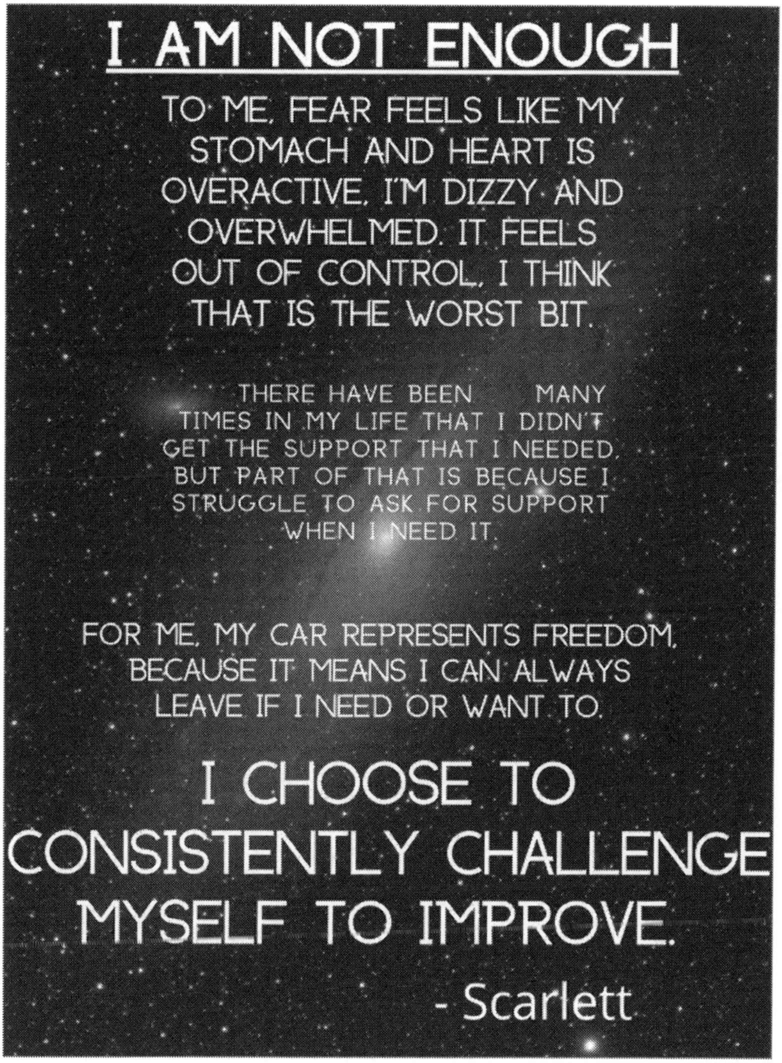
I AM NOT ENOUGH
TO ME, FEAR FEELS LIKE MY STOMACH AND HEART IS OVERACTIVE, I'M DIZZY AND OVERWHELMED. IT FEELS OUT OF CONTROL, I THINK THAT IS THE WORST BIT.
THERE HAVE BEEN MANY TIMES IN MY LIFE THAT I DIDN'T GET THE SUPPORT THAT I NEEDED, BUT PART OF THAT IS BECAUSE I STRUGGLE TO ASK FOR SUPPORT WHEN I NEED IT.
FOR ME, MY CAR REPRESENTS FREEDOM, BECAUSE IT MEANS I CAN ALWAYS LEAVE IF I NEED OR WANT TO.
I CHOOSE TO CONSISTENTLY CHALLENGE MYSELF TO IMPROVE.
- Scarlett

# DEALING WITH CHALLENGES

Be it emotional
Be it physical
Be it mental
Be it spiritual
When the challenges come

I Breath in YH
I breath out WH
YHWH
My emotion calm
My body relaxes
My brain processes
My heart opens

YHWH
The challenge less threatening
Now I can respond rather than react

—KYLA

What represents freedom?

# EVOLVED

When I stop and think what freedom truly means to me I have to stop and take a breath. I say that 'cause having freedom takes my breath away. It is so beautiful. Freedom to me is not being totally confined to my own mind. Being so imprisoned by the chaos around me. Freedom is choosing to get up each day and live, not just because I am still breathing but because it's my choice to live. Freedom is being sober sorting through all of the things that have been my prison, the feelings that have held me hostage have true meaning now. I know what they stand for and in knowing that I found true peace. Freedom from my addict allowed me to find me, to love me and to live free. So to me freedom comes from within...

—KRISTIE

# FREEDOM

The ability to be me, unjudged.
Not represented as an x-con but as a human Becoming...

Allowed to thrive and grow with the limitations put upon me by those who's unsavory acts have not yet been exposed.
True freedom for me represents the renewing of my mind and the inner strength to manifest my dreams into reality.
-Coming soon near you-

—ANONYMOUS

Create the light and darkness
that you carry in your life.

# CLOUD PIECE

Looking up at the evening sky
To keep the tears from my eye
I notice strange shaped clouds
Sharp and jagged edges
Like a Chinese dragon
In a parade
Blinking tears away
I see clearly
The sharp jagged clouds
Become feathered wings
Outspread in flight
A round, gray-bottomed cloud below
The body
Whispering of the body
A head
My illusion of a dragon
Becomes a dove in flight
Bringing hope and light

—WENONA

# THE DARKNESS AND LIGHT THAT I CARRY

Darkness like the loyalest of all friends sits with me, walks with me, sleeps with me, breathes with me and no matter what, never lets me go.

I know of no other life

I have no other loyal friends like this.

When we fall out, I shine for a day or two. I feel invincible. I move mountains, redecorate my house, spend all of my earnings on new clothes, I dye my hair and even join a gym.

But my BFF pulls me right back, where I obviously belong and we drink and we smoke cigarettes, stay up all night and party. Hard.

I wake up hungover, Monday morning knocks on the door, one kid other kid, fucking stupid dog SHE bought me to make me feel loved needs a crap, my coffee is spilt, its raining outside, I can't find my bloody car keys, personal trainer sends inspirational bullshit memes of how inspiring our session is going to be today, I light up a cigarette, I inhale and exhale and there she is, sexy as ever, on my very own sofa, feet up, in her low octave husky voice says "Morning," makes a genious sarcastic joke about my training and we laugh and flirt and I am taken by her and am all hers. Again. She is my BFF after all. The one who never leaves my side.

CUT TO LIGHT

xxxxxxxxxxxxxxxxxxxxxxxxxxxxxxxxxxxxxxxxxxxxxxxxxx

I am happy. I am productive. I have friends wishing to have my life, my body, my face, my hair, my career, my husband, my talent. I am the one who always finds time for stuff that matters. Even if it is at inconvenient times (wink wink). I am that friend who will go to war for your happiness and lose limbs, bleed out but WIN, bringing your enemies head on the plate which I'd drop to your feet. The one who lives for the moment, laughs at her own farts, lets kids run free and speak their truth as much as it hurts to hear it. I apologize to them on a daily basis. They are the source of my light, (my BFF has an issue with this.)

## CONCLUSION

xxxxxxxxxxxxxxxxxxxxxxxxxxxxxxxxxxxxxxxxxxxxxxxxxxxx

I blamed it on my father.

I blamed it on the war

I blamed it on my poverty and refuge

I blamed it on my mother

I blamed it on my husband

It was everyone's fault.

But my own.

Only BFF understood.

I looked for the missing love in the most unusual places.

The search still continues, and you know what? Due to it I have traveled the world, learnt languages, welcomed other cultures, ate some of the most exceptional foods, kissed some of the most extraordinary men, portrayed some of the most admirable characters on established stages across the globe.

I carry both. It's which you feed most is the one that grows the most. So be careful. One might outgrow the other and you'll find disbalance. But just like the ying yang, heaven and hell, piano keys, bride and groom, zebra crossing, chess board, black and white movies, this very white document with black letters on, or my very own eyes.....One cannot exist without the other.

It's the price we pay for calling ourselves human. So don't beat yourself too much about it. Even the all smiley perfect bitch of a face colleague sitting right next to you in the office, has her own BBF truuuuuust meeeeee, she is just hiding it better.

Relax. Do what ever fucking feels right to you.

Those who don't get it aren't your tribe anyhow.

Live for YOU. Dab into the dark, cry it out, fuck it out, drink it out, smoke it out.

Then find your light and shine

For as brief as it may be.

Shine 100 percent.

No guilt.

Just glow.

That's where the answers are.

For as brief as it may be.

Just like our time on earth.

—MIA ZARA

—PAIGE HARRISON

# YELLOW NOT BLUE

Some days are cold and dark
I struggle to make a mark
I feel like a ship lost at sea
Destined to wander aimlessly.

Then there are days
When everything goes a different way
I find myself happy to be
Like the sun is shining just for me.

The brighter days are always ahead
While the dark ones are left behind
At night while in bed
Tricks are played on me by my own mind.

Most days I try to achieve all goals I set for myself
But sadly many goals
Get left on the shelf, to collect dust
Even though I know they're a must.

All I hear is advice
Given my many different voices
A lot was sacrificed
But life is full of choices.

So what do I do
I pursue mental health
So I can be yellow
Not blue.

—BETHNEY THOMAS

# LIGHT OR DARK

The light experiences and the dark experiences I carry.

The light me and the dark me I carry.

The light and dark in the world that I carry.

Being in the mountains with the trees and grass and rivers, noticing the things happening there, is a good experience that is both darkness and light. Things happen in the raw world of woodland creatures: mothering, also disease and gory death. I see that it is we who have decided there is such a thing as good and evil, and only we who can be.

The curve of my son's cheek or my daughter's eyelashes: those children are light itself; parenting them is full of the darkness of regret and uncertainty.

The me that has eaten less, walked more, laughed, and taken my supplements, likes that the way is easier. But when I feel heavy and dull and mean anyway, can I reject myself? It's then that I need more love.

The good on the great human proscenium of world events seems both light and dark, both beautiful. The evil seems both light and dark; both ugly. I groan as the evil seems to swell. I cheer for the good I

Sometimes trust will overcome it. But how would there be a story

without teams?

A duality that comes from reality—there is empty space
or there is light.

But before there were eyes, what did each mean?

I try to see without eyes. I try to love both teams.

I try to hold my darkness and my light with even attention.

—ATIENO

# DARKNESS AND LIGHT

Darkness can be very beautiful or very sad.
The darkness I am most fond of is the desert night sky.
The sky is so clear you can see all of the stars and know that
you are so small yet the sweet peace you feel makes it all feel so good.
The darkness inside of me is the mourning, sadness,
pain, panic, fear of the unknown, and worry.
It is very lonely there, so alone, a kind of isolation and cold I would
never wish on another soul to feel.

For the past 7 years I have known these feelings all too well.
In the beginning, it felt as if I could choke on them, suffocate
within the pain.
As each year has passed it has lightened the weight of the
darkness a little.
But it still remains lying in wait....

Light can be very beautiful and also so bright it is blinding.
A different type of pain.
The light of the morning sun pouring through the window.
A filling of sunlight and joy that wells up and expands to
overflowing.
My favorite memories of the light of the sun is back
home in Southern California. The summer sun, so warm it's like a
big hug that wraps its arms around you, filling my soul until it's
overflowing.

The light within me comes from the center of my being
and is all encompassing. It is every fiber of my being, every cell.
My light is bright when allowed to be—inextinguishable.

I feel this intimidates some people which causes me to pull
back and hide or dampen the light.
Others seem to know that I can see by this light, things
other people don't want to be seen.
This too can rob and steal my light, leaving me in the dark.
I refuse to no longer allow myself to live my life for others anymore.
What brings me joy, happiness, and makes
my light shine, I will do as much as possible.
Shine, light, shine.

—MICHELLE

# 2%

Darkness is the fuel that I use, the depression I've abused, and the light I give others
Darkness is choosing to put myself in the view of rapist, thieves, and liars, pretending I wouldn't drown from addiction and I wouldn't turn out as the same before me
Darkness is abandoning my daughter, watching her thrash for me, and walking away anyway because I couldn't let go of heroin
Darkness is knowing and wanting to be a good mother, but it's not enough
Stealing from people I love and feeling betrayed when they turned me in
Dark clarity creeps in through the small moments of abstinence, I feel I've had enough but my body's convulsing and throwing up in a jail cell floor alone
Darkness is feeling scared I won't ever get out of this mess, the longer my mind isn't clouded the more I can see the light
Light is the moment when I felt I had a fighting chance, the weekend visits with my daughter and the weeds she would pull in the facility to keep moms prison home pretty

### Darkness, Guilt, Shame

Light is remembering I can't live back there
and continuing to heal my life
Light is getting out of prison and achieving my goals, celebrating
each year I get my family, beating statistic after statistic
Light is paying forward, having family gatherings at my house,
and family trusting me with their children
Light is making amends for the things I can, and living
a better life for the things I can't
Light is having my children learn to trust my consistency
Darkness created my light, I am the 2%

—CAROLINE

# MYSTERY

Does darkness chase away light? Or does light chase away darkness?

In all the dark situations I have experienced, I will still choose light because the dark felt dark.

There is mystery in darkness, beauty in light.

I have had moments of darkness, sad dark thoughts, things that have happened to me, things I did and what I fear might happen, but I'm glad in my head the light overpowers the darkness.

There is mystery in darkness and beauty in light.

The fear starts when we are little, when you call to your mum not to switch off the lights before we sleep. It's dark when we close our eyes, but we are still afraid of the dark, fearing the unknown.

It can be a very dark night but the stars will make the darkest night beautiful.

I appreciate the mystery of the dark things I have felt, kept to myself and from others to judge but still I choose to walk in light.

I also have felt the most beautiful things with my eyes closed in the dark.

There is mystery in darkness, beauty in light.

—FUNGAI

# UNDER THE WINGS OF GOD

I chose to remain under the wings of God.

Allowing God to renew my mind and strength constantly.

The biggest challenge I ever had to face were my own thoughts.

Thoughts to love and not hate.

To give and not take.

To accept even views and imperfection

And celebrate the differences.

Remembering that we all fall short

But the darkness will never overpower

The light.

—TANUIA DAVIS

# BECOMING

I crowned
I cooed
I crowed
I rose
I fought the pauper
In a golden robe.
Fighting
Lightly
Fearing
Lighting
I sat in a dark
And vain abode.
I am
The will
The want
The waiting
The Queen
Of mental masturbating.
I ditched the dream
And bought a brain
I skinned the lion
And burned his mane.
I molded milk

And milked the mother
I burned the beast
And bore his brother.
I built
I bought
I sought
I sold
I left my longing
In the cold
Crippled
Crying
Multiplying
My longing
Loose
And scared of dying.
I dreamt
I drove
Derailed
I died.
A dead man laughed
A story lied
A fault line cracked
The planets sighed,
I fought the light
But darkness cried.

—MEGHAN

# LIFT ME UP

Suspended moments in time.
Transitions, some great and some small.
The family that grew and taught us all more than we knew—

The etchings of a year, of a life,
The tears that fell on the basement floor and across the front porch,
The laughter heard through the floorboards and bouncing off the trampoline,
The back deck: the place of contemplation and gathering as kids shot off the slip n slide over and over and over again.

The swapped clothing, cold pizza, and coffees handed off in doorways,
The knowing smiles of getting through yet another day.
The feelings we baked into things...

And how we all learnt to make something new work.

These are the days of discovery,
of warped time and flexibility like we've never known,

These are the days of being taught more than I teach.

These are the days I'll remember, fresh in my mind, soft in my eyes, open in my heart.

—NIKKI WEAVER

# LIGHT AND DARK

I mistook my lightness for darkness due to other people's idea of light.
I tried to fit into all shades of white and slept most comfortably closer to gray.does that make me colourblind? blind is the last word I'd use when describing myself. I see. . I see. I see best without the eyes. I see . I also see more than I should..
Darkness comes from not living your truth. From honoring nurture, beliefs, tradition, caring more of other people's opinion and perception of you. Fitting into the boxes of normal. Who's normal? Their normal or my normal? Normal is an illusion. What's normal for the spider is a chaos for the fly. Yet the most admired artists are praised for seeing the world differently. They are awarded for their darkness. Best music, lyrics, poetry come from the same area of gray. So, if it's dominant in your life at the moment, use it. Express it. Please bear in mind it does not need to transfer to light. I beg you not to turn it to light prematurely . Live it, let it consume every atom of your body so when the true light does shine in you recognize it.
My light is on its way. And I am ok that her arrival time is now way overdue.

—MIA

# MOVING FORWARD

What lies about myself do I need
to let go of?

# LOST GIRL

Find yourself I hear them say
The parts of you that went away
Left scarred and broken from the past
Let it go it wasn't meant to last
Bitter, hurting, bruised and used
Those are feelings you must lose
Dry your eyes, wipe away those tears
It's time to free you from your fears
Place yourself on bended knee
All your hopelessness not set it free
Search to remember who you wanted to be
Broken dreams and wishes too
Let them all flow back to you
Just close your eyes and you will see
All That you were meant to be

—ANONYMOUS

# REOCCURRING THOUGHTS

I often experience change in relationships as a form of rejection. Most likely stemming from past trauma, when people naturally choose to move on or change the relationship we currently have, my walls go up as a defense mechanism to avoid any type of hurt. I allow myself to get close to people, and pour all my heart into them. Then if they move on, the lie that I begin to believe is that they are rejecting ME. Which may or may not be true. It's a deeply rooted insecurity to surround myself with people who are amazing, so either they make me look good, OR, the attention is completely off of me and the responsibility to "perform", is on them. As I get older, and even just more recently, I recognized this in myself and vowed to change this pattern. I want to know and believe wholeheartedly that at my core, I am deeply loved, gifted, and called. Anyone who stands with me, or beside me, even just for a season, is not for ME. It's for them and for others to benefit from.

—LINDSAY

# THE LIES

Throughout my life I've heard people say so

many nasty things that I have grabbed hold of.

The one I truly hung onto is "I will never change"

"I'll always be a drug addict".

For a long time I lived there.

I gave people ammunition to talk like that about me.

The sad thing is I was so far stuck in my addiction I believed what people said.

I feel like just maybe I broke myself down.

I beat myself up, always allowing the defeat of my addiction to be winning.

Well I believed it all until about 2.5 years ago.

I've been sober by choice. I am making life changes.

I am a new woman today. I am different and today nobody

can say those things about me…

Because I can change and I did change.

SO those lies…

I have buried them because today…

I AM CHANGE.

—KRISTIE

# UNWORTHY

The main lie I have believed about myself most of my life is that I am unworthy of love. I think this seed was planted when I was very young. My father was an alcoholic, emotionally unavailable and sometimes violent. He would watch me during the day while my mother worked, but I really felt ignored and unimportant. I guess he assumed I knew he loved me simply because he was present, but I didn't. I felt like a burden and a nuisance. I loved him very much; in fact, I adored him. All I wanted was for him to hold and play with me, but he kept me at a distance, and because he was sometimes emotionally unpredictable, I also kept myself there.

I know now he himself felt unworthy of love. This is the family demon that has been passed onto me. My dad has been dead for 14 years. He took several strong pain killers, and an aneurism in his heart exploded. I got to experience his love for ten years before his death. He had sobered up, but later became addicted to painkillers instead. He was only 45. His early death left a hole in my heart.

I continued to believe I was unworthy of love, despite having evidence to the contrary. My mother nurtured me, my kids adored me, but as I started to sink into addiction I started to push them away. I didn't want to hurt them as my dad did to me.

I took pain pills to escape reality and numb the pain. I started seeing men who were abusive alcoholics just like my dad . The more men mistreated me, the more I confirmed my worst fear. I was broken down, and the real me slipped away. I started using meth with my last boyfriend which led to me losing my children, and committing a terrible rovery. I kept "losing" the people that loved me. Everything surrounding me just wanted to use me. All these things kept confirming the lir beheld I was unlovable. But I was doing this. I was making this happen.

I never expected anyone to treat me right. I knew eventually the men I was with would leave me. I thought the things they did to me were a reflection of who I was and in essence, you are, giving them the power to determine that. Putting that kind of power into the wrong hands is very dangerous. You may give yourself to someone who will selfishley use you for their own purpose.

No one is perfect. No one loves perfectly. And most of these people who use and abuse others have a warped sense of what love is. Love in itself is unconditional, but when someone attaches all their baggage love is robbed of all its innocence. People out there need to understand that letting the wrong people in our lives can make you believe you are undeserving of love. This is not something we are meant to think about ourselves. We were made to love. It is our design. When someone hurts you, puts you down, rejects, or abandons you , you may begin to believe this lie, but it has nothing to do with you. It is an abuser's own hurt and pains being projected onto you. The fact they can hurt you confirms that they are loved for them but it robs you of your own love for yourself.

I have done a lot of healing in prison and my perspective has changed. I now know that the lack of love I had was for myself. I accomplished much in my life before the drugs. Before prison I had three beautiful children, was a doting mother, went to college, got a degree and worked different occupations that interested me. Even then, when I achieved almost everything I set out to do I never thought I was enough. But that was a lie and it was my own self destructive path that made it seem true.

Even though I see that now, it still comes up from time to time. I have to remind myself that this belief is a result of my childhood trauma; not truth. I've come to understand that there is a God, that he loves me and I've done nothing to deserve it, It's just there. I know my father loved me, He just didn't know how to express it right. But most importantly, I love myself. Just because I am human and make mistakes does not mean I'm unworthy of love. That is the beauty of love. It is freely given despite worth and I make a conscious choice to give it to myself.

My children are back in my life, and they tell me all the time they love me, and I know they do. Even though I'm in prison, people display their love daily in the kind of gestures they do. I see it now. But I would not if I didn't love myself, and that is what changes everything.

—CRYSTAL

What haven't you said?

# QUESTION

Can it be that everything is connected by invisible energy?

Everything that happens creates paths to certain individuals or life experiences that are needed to open up our mind. And what if our minds aren't willing to be opened, what then? Do we seep into anger and depression? Unwilling to find the truth in our experience? Do we go down into a stage of despair with only moments of clarity, that try to guide us back to the bigger picture of life? And what of the people who are overly happy or strangely disconnected from the pain of life, what happens to them? Do they live in a box inside their mind filing away negative emotions and thoughts?

Surely one day that Box will overflow and come crashing down? Can it be that life is at a constant state of trying to create balance?

—CAROLINE

# 2020

Devastation,
Pandemic
Police brutality
Protests & Riots
Across the world

What has this year come to?

I turn on the T.V
To see...
This virus has claimed
Hundreds of lives,
There's another
Protest downtown
Tear gas released
Fires set
And
Windows broken
Nobodies safe

What's that I hear
Level 3 evacuation
Being ordered
Grab what you can
And go

Some fair better than others
And those less fortunate
Are left to rebuild
And start anew

As is all this devastation
Wasn't enough
We have children
Feeling strain
And taking their
Own lives.

Trump or Biden?
Now it's time to vote
For a better 2021
and stand with
And hand up
Instead of a
Hand out...

—MORGAN

# THEY

They cant see the many pathways;
Long nights clutching my sheets,
birds resting on my shoulders.
Screaming long tones of expectations unmet.
Creative escape games on the long trailer; or is it a boat?

They. Who are they today?
My children can't see my constant drive hidden by stress lines
and clear glasses.
Drive to push and separate the constant algorithms of choice
and effect.
Past to our present, my life to theirs.

Who are they besides humans?
Who do I want to see?
I'll just put the mirrors in front of me.
What you see is you, what I see is me.

—ANONYMOUS

# THE WAR INSIDE MY HEART

"Who am I?" is an important question
Although, sometimes it's more like, "Who am I today?"

I unravel the trauma from my past only to find
someone underneath
that I hardly know

I observe those around me,
those I want to be like,
but I feel like
I am nothing like them

I blame my past,
but my past made me
Ever changing, there's still hope

I rewrite my story,
but it comes out the same.
I try again.
and again.

Then realize I am the sum of all of my rough drafts.
A girl just trying to write her autobiography
with a pen
who wishes she had a pencil.

I meet another Author and
realize I am not alone

They tell me my story will find a place in this library
as long as I keep writing
and so I keep writing.

—MAKAILA

# THE POWER OF REFRAME

| OLD BELIEFS | NEW BELIEFS |
|---|---|
| I need to teach others a lesson | It is not my job to teach others anything |
| Things have to be done my way | Everyone has their own way of doing things |
| I know better because I am a woman | Men can do house work just as well |
| I need to yell to be heard | Yelling is abusive and people tune it out |
| Using shame or guilt is ok to get my way | Shaming is not ok and abusive |
| Physical discipline is the only way to get through to some children | Physical discipline only works temporarily, and destroys children's spirit |
| Problems need to be solved on the spot | It is ok to table a conversation to avoid abuse |
| Leaving an argument or taking a time out shows weakness | Taking time out is responsible, it shows self-awareness and strength. |
| Children do not have the right to boundaries | Children have the same rights to their feelings and boundaries as adults |
| Abuse is ok if it gets me my way | Abuse is never ok |

| | |
|---|---|
| Abuse is relative to cultural | Culture is an excuse, and there are NO EXCUSES |
| Fear equals respect | Fear is abusive and one loses respect from it |
| Self Defense is not abuse | Abuse does not excuse abuse |
| I can use abuse to teach a lesson | Abuse is never ok! Natural consequences teach lessons |
| I must be perfect and must expect perfectionism from my children | Only God is perfect, and I have given permission to myself to not be perfect |
| Interrupting will get people to hear me | Interrupting is controlling and abusive |
| I do not need to let the others finish their thoughts. If I know what they are going to say I can interrupt to save time. | Everyone has the right to communicate and be heard without being interrupted. |
| My needs are more important | Everyone is important, we are all God's children |
| Lying or manipulating is ok if I get my way | Manipulation is controlling and abusive |
| My time is more valuable than others | Lying is abusive and can hide abuse, the truth sets us free |
| Being late is relative to culture and it no big deal | Being late is a controlling behavior, and disrespectful to others, whose time is just as valuable. |

—IOANNA

What do you believe in?

# FAITH

I believe in…

God, Jesus and the Holy Spirit

The power of Love and Kindness

That there are still loyal, honest and truly good people…they're just more difficult to find.

Karma. The good and bad that we put out into the Universe always makes its way back to us eventually… We get what we give.

I keep telling myself

"I don't care, just give up."

But that's a lie…

I do care, that's why

I continue to get up

instead of just giving up.

—TAUSHA

# THE ROOT

It brings me comfort in knowing
the root of all our problems
is buried within us

Why that bothers us,
Why do we feel the way we feel?
We are both the problems
and the answers.

Only we know the secret to our own happiness.
If we will only dig deep enough to discover it

How far would you go
to find your own happiness?
What would you give?
What would you give up?
Who would you meet along the way,
and what would they teach you?

The root determines the amount of life that we carry into the world

It is where all of us connect
to ourselves
and to everything else.
What if we made life about caring for our root?

Then we would all blossom
the ways
colors
shapes
we were meant to.

—MAKAILA DICKSON

# REASON

I believe in giving everyone the benefit of the doubt. To understand and allow for strength and weakness. Trusting God and myself to accomplish the work we have both started in my life. I believe that without some form of mistake or set back one can never truly know what it means to be free. I believe in God, Second chances, family, friends, and fun. I believe my steps are ordained by God and NOT Man.

—TANULA

# BELIEVE

I believe in God, and His very real and present love for me. I believe in having faith, especially in times where you can't see two feet in front of you. I believe in real, unconditional love. I believe in forgiveness. I believe that you can have peace in the midst of a storm. I believe that pain and suffering are a part of the process & can be used for something beautiful. I believe that there is more to this life to be born, just to exist, and die. I believe we've been created on purpose. I believe there is more for us besides just life on earth. I believe in the goodness of God, and that even at our worst, God sees our best. I believe that there is still good in this world. I believe that God has called me to be light and life to a younger generation, giving them hope.

—LINDSAY

# INSIDE SELF LOVE

Write yourself a future love letter

# A THOUSAND TEARS

The two trees laid an unhinged path to you.
Yielding only to my phantom—as your guest.
The zephyrs of love hold true,
Pulling the threads that reeve my haunted psyche.
Temptation was the bully of a silver-tongued (Clio?), or
The sharpened rasp of Themis' daughter,
One to sing our past—one to abrupt our destiny.
Both a harbinger. An Amaranth.        My name is Shade.
I'd been hoodwinked in the sin of carnal flesh,
Taking what I wanted and leaving them boneless.
My soul once a nomad, living amongst the satyrs,
To sustain my earthly needs—as their host.
Then, a vagabond of society alone and isolated for eternity,
Vacillating from my soul's unrelinquished quest.
Bearing the quietness of its emptiness,
indulging in the hollowness of my grief.
I've worn the cloak of a knave—a pitiless rogue with children.
Driven by my own stained childhood.
Raised by the wolf and outcast by its alpha.
My ambitions lost to bacchanal feasts of consciousness,
This drive facilitated by the pull of our tether.
The pulsing tug and manipulation of slumbering echoes.
A serendipitous chance my voice carries on the back of
fog and shadows.
Swiftly past a thousand tears, a thousand memories,
A thousand tears.

—PAIGE

# MIREYA

Know this, you have gone through some shit you didn't EVER think you could get through. You're stronger than you think. Take it a bit at a time.

Even if you have to take a step back and take time for yourself, DO IT!

It's okay to feel the way you feel, just remember to get back up, let it go. Move on or in some cases make a difference. Your voice does matter, and you can choose to make that difference. Know not everyday is going to be great, and that's okay because those storms aren't forever either. Love the good and bad times because they both teach you something. Knowing it makes you strong, asking for help when you can't do it all yourself. Imagine the growth in relationships that will happen. Love, forgive, and do both of these for yourself too! Tomorrow isn't promised, which isn't bad, it just means enjoy the present moment!

Love yourself,

MIREYA

# TANUIA

We finally made it. This has been a very long road we have traveled.

One situation after the next. One problem or another. We never gave up though.

We have a rockin' support group. The women and men in our life love us very much. We can depend on them and they can depend on us. Our faith in God grows stronger every day. I truly believe that God has set us free. No hurt, habit, or hand up can stop us from being successful. We have everything back 100 fold. Family, finances, education and advocating for others as well. Let's not stop here. Keep moving forward. Remember Tanuia, it's not what's at the top of the hill as much as it is the climb. You said it yourself. "There's no excuse not to grow."

### Mission Statement to Self:

As I strive for success I will not lose sight of how valuable I am as a person.

Faith, family, and education are but a part of my core values.

Continuously learning strategies to overcome obstacles that might otherwise trip me up.

I have built a strong support system. This has allowed me to both give and receive.

By standing on these principles and staying true to my faith, I have learned to enjoy everyday life abundantly.

Love,

TANUIA

# DEAR SELF

I am writing you this letter to encourage you to do the things to see you through.
When in doubt...
Find faith in yourself. There is nothing in life that you can't do, as long as you put your mind to it.
When feeling alone...
Look up to your higher power, who is beside you. Just call on him by name.
When feeling weak...
Never give up. With all that happened in the past it has taken a strong woman to have made it through.
When feeling ugly...
Keep your head up. You are a beautiful individual. True beauty lies within.
When feeling unworthy...
Remember to forgive yourself. Otherwise things will weigh us down.
When feeling down...
Remember you've got people that care about you and want to see you succeed.
And when you feel you have had enough and just feel like giving up...
Pick yourself up again. Dust yourself off, continue to move through it.
It is then that you will find true power WITHIN.

Love,

EVA

# DEAR KRISTIE

There is so much to be said, I'll start with just a few things. First you are growing into such a beautiful woman. The broken you from before is fading away into the past. I know the struggle has become so real for you not knowing how to handle these new emotions from within. This is the first time to face your demons sober. You are one of the strongest women I know. You have come so far. A survivor of so many things. I never thought you would get to a place where the woman looking back in the mirror was really your best friend. Remember as you grow to treat yourself kind, respect all of your decisions, most of all love yourself and embrace the woman you are becoming.

I love you Kristie, I mean it truly. Proceed with caution you are still fragile.

Love,

KRISTIE

# INCARCERATED WOMEN

## Coffee Creek Correctional Facility, Oregon

Unnoticed - Kristie

Twisted Truths - Tanya

Why Try - Tanuia

Silent Kisses - Morgan

A time of no support - Kristie

Prison - Kyla

Frozen - Megan

Fear feels like - Michelle

Trepidation - Mireya

Still. - Tanya

Within the Struggle - Michelle F.

There's no excuse not to grow - Tanuia

I can see now - Anonymous

Dealing with Challenges - Kyla

Freedom - Anonymous

Evolved - Kristie

Cloud piece - Wenona

Yellow not Blue - Bethany

Darkness and light - Michelle

Under the wings of God - Tanuia

Lost Girl - Anonymous

The Lies - Kristie

Unworthy - Crystal

2020 - Morgan

Faith - Tausha

Reason - Tanuia

A Thousand Tears - Paige

Mireya - Mireya

Tanuia - Tanuia

Dear Self - Eva

Dear Kristie - Kristie

### Images

Crying Eyes - Summer.George

Untitled - Paige.Harrison

# NOT INCARCERATED WOMEN

Uncertain - Miranda

Mantra - Anonymous

Strength - Anonymous

Chaos - Anonymous

I am Not enough - Scarlett

Light or Dark - Atieno

2% - Caroline (Formerly Incarcerated)

Mystery - Fungia

Lift me up - Nikki

Becoming - Meghan

The darkness and light that I carry - Mia

Light and Dark - Mia

Reoccurring Thoughts - Lindsay

Question - Caroline

They - Anonymous

The War Inside My Heart - Makaila (Formerly Incarcerated)

The Power of Reframe - Ioanna

The Root - Makaila

Believe - Lindsay

# JOIN THE JOURNEY

In 2020 the world was turned upside down for many of us. On The Inside went from teaching in person to women in prison, to wondering how we could continue to support and contribute positively to the women we serve with no contact. We began to send in weekly newsletters to the women with personal experiences, poetry, and prompts. They could respond to the prompt pen pal style, and we offered our support in this way. We started to run a virtual class series for women with the hopes to somehow co collaborate. When we can find the similarities we all carry, rather than the differences we can support each other's healing. These are the prompts and the framework to our journey through the pandemic. We invite you to join our journey and follow the prompts. The guidelines are to respond in whatever way you feel moved to do so: poetry, writing, drawing, painting, photography ext.

# PROMPTS

"Is there one belief or recurring thought that you can release in order to cultivate more self-healing?"

"What is a time in your life that you didn't get the support you needed?"

"What does fear look or feel like?"

"What in your life do you choose to challenge?"

"What represents freedom?"

"Create the light and darkness that you carry in your life"

"What lies about myself do I need to let go of?"

"What haven't you said?"

"What do you believe in?"

"Write yourself a future love letter"

# OUR BOARD OF DIRECTORS

We asked our board members to each answer two questions: "When I think about being incarcerated I imagine" and "I choose to serve with On The Inside because…".

## CAROLINE COX

I don't have to imagine being incarcerated because I was incarcerated. What I remember is the lack of support, counseling, and opportunity to heal. I remember not being able to hug another woman, always feeling like I had to keep my guard up. I remember the moment that I decided I would not let prison be a waste of my time, especially when the time was going to cause further trauma to my daughter. I had to make it worth it, and I did.

I serve with On The Inside because it has become the foundation of my purpose so far in life. I found a reason for all the muck of my past to somehow pay it forward and change the legacy I will leave behind.

## TINA PACKER

When I think about being incarcerated these are the things that come up for me: what did I do that put me in this place? Am I dangerous to my family and fellow citizens? Do they (and who is "they"?) think that punishment will somehow right my "sins" or is it inflicting more pain all around me? Does being controlled teach me anything? Are my two feelings of shame and rage conducive to living a conscious life? Or am I stuck here?

I choose to serve on the Board of On The Inside because it forces me to look at the way we treat people who have "transgressed"; because I am curious about the way creativity can find a way through despair and anger; and how there but for the grace of circumstance go I.

## ATIENO BIRD

When I think about being incarcerated I imagine ... the inner strength it would take every moment.

I choose to serve with On The Inside because ... I believe art and community heal us, and we all deserve healing; because I would need this lifeline if I were on the inside; and because it is a privilege to "be let in" and connect with women, anywhere.

## KAREN PRIDE

When I think about being incarcerated I imagine the difficulty in reaching deep to connect to my inner strength, which I know I would need in order to navigate the incarceration period.

I choose to serve with On The Inside because they are offering tools to help those who are incarcerated find, engage with and expand their inner strength.

## MEGAN GAFFNEY

When I think about being incarcerated I imagine grappling to accept the injustice inherent in our prison system. I imagine yearning for those I love and miss on the outside. I imagine striving to build communities within these walls of confinement, to abate loneliness. I imagine time to reflect but little silence in which to do so, a slowing of time, a blurring of self.

I seek ways to use the random privilege of the white skin and middle class life I was born to to build equity in a world rife with injustice. I believe in creative expression as the greatest path to freedom and when I consider women confined inside, I fervently hope that an opportunity to express themselves might offer some moments of freedom. I feel the connection of sisterhood in communities of women, though I know we may be divided individually by race, class, sexuality, in aspects of our gender identities, still we share the experience of walking through this world as women, in all its gifts and sorrows and in all its complexity. Finally, I will follow Nikki Weaver to the ends of the Earth and this organization. born of her beautiful heart and soul, in her capable, loving hands, is bound to make meaningful change.

## MARIE GONZALEZ

When I think about being incarcerated, I imagine not being seen as the person I am, but rather of the crime convicted.

I choose to serve On The Inside because in a world where we are constantly reminded of our differences, the work of On The Inside creates connections and facilitates healing by, in part, reminding us that we are more alike than we are different.

## BECK THOMPSON

When I think about being incarcerated I imagine feeling trapped, feeling like my freedom and my livelihood were taken away and I can imagine that it would take great strength to make it through.

I choose to serve with On The Inside because the work is so important for the world and I have seen the change to the women on the inside which has a ripple effect on the whole planet. This work is vital for the world right now and there is no better feeling than watching it grow!

## KATIE MORELL

When I think about being incarcerated I imagine the solitude. The isolation. The yearning for connection. The constant need for self-love and reminding myself that I, no matter what, am worthy of love.

I choose to serve with On The Inside because I believe that everyone deserves to live a life that feels good to them, no matter their circumstances. That everyone deserves for their voice to be heard. That each person isn't a prison to their circumstances or their pasts. That every person deserves love and deserves to exist in this world. I believe in listening to stories, and that all stories matter.

## MIA ZARA

When I think about being incarcerated I imagine walls. Barriers or space and time. Vacant voices, monotone colors, undercooked meals and overcooked thoughts. Fading memories of what once was happiness without appreciation. Disappearing details of a loved ones face like a watercolor portrait left on the porch in the rain.

I serve with On The Inside because I am a human with faults a many. I serve to help deal with pain. There are many pains which hurt in a similar way. Each and everyone of us carries it in silence. Like an embarrassed secret. Mine is equal to others. Others are equal to mine. I serve to process and understand pain in order to see beauty in everyday life hidden in most unusual places. One only needs to want to recognise it and help those around to see it too.

## DR. NYEPUDZAYI MERCY NYANGULU

When I think about being incarcerated I imagine being cut off, feeling lonely, locked up, de-humanized, despised, worthless, valueless, and unwanted.

I choose to serve with On The Inside because I would like to make in a small way the difference for those sisters on the inside by bringing hope for a normal future, by keeping in touch with reality and keeping in touch with those sisters on the outside through various training and programs being taken inside facilities.

## ELENA BROWER

When I think about being incarcerated I imagine needing the support of women who are truly listening, in order to process and integrate my experience and actually learn from it.

I choose to serve with On The Inside because I feel somehow connected to the women serving time; it could be any one of us and my wish is simply to help bring some light and warmth to their lives.

## CINDY LONE

When I think about being incarcerated I imagine not having freedom as a choice. Where I have to relive a bad choice from the past on the daily and continue doing so well into the unforeseen future.

I serve with On The Inside because it's one tiny way I can affect change in a world where big change is urgently required.

## LISA COLLINS

When I think about being incarcerated I imagine ... the struggle of self-love and forgiveness or the thought others may forget about me.

I choose to serve with On The Inside because ... God loves us all and our only job is to care for one another which is everyone. I long to heal our world and provide love and care to all I can. On The Inside are the legs to this work of collective care and well-being.

### JAZMIN JIMENEZ

When I think about being incarcerated I imagine a feeling of "othering" which does not honor the full human dignity which every person deserves.

I choose to serve with On The Inside because it chooses love over fear. It chooses to break down the "us/them" dichotomy and see us as just "us" through art, storytelling and relationship building. I love the way OTI challenges everyone who comes to the circle to bring her truest self to the work- with all our beauty and bruises. OTI holds an authentic space for inclusion which is needed in today's divided world more than ever. I am grateful for the friendships and connections that have been born with the birth of OTI and I can't wait to see what the future holds for the organization- the sky's the limit!

## FUNGAI

When I think about being incarcerated I imagine small spaces, routine, different personalities, no freedom to make simple decisions on what I want to wear, the time to have my meal or when to soak in the warm sunlight. I see small windows in my head and little light, I imagine endless corridors and uniformed guards. I imagine craving for freedom and wishing I was a bird. I think of how lonely someone could be in a room full of people. I imagine seeing sad eyes and hearing background laughter..

I choose to serve with On the Inside because I choose to believe that incarceration should only be physical. I want to help free the mind... I want to inspire and I want to touch hearts. I want to hear laughter and see eyes sparkle .. I want women to forget where they are even if it's for an hour.

I want to serve not judge, we want to dance, create, write and embody.. I want the women inside to look forward to something.